Air Fryer Cookbook:

A simple and amazing guide to delicious air frying recipes

James Hughes

ISBN: 1979461023
ISBN-13: 9781979461023

CONTENTS

1 INTRODUCTION

Buying an air fryer is one of the best things I've ever done – and, if you ask other owners, they'll tell you how much they love their machine too.

I'll be honest. I was worried at first that it would end up in the back of the cupboard, along with the other kitchen gadgets I've been given for Christmas over the years; the waffle makers; the cupcake makers; the crepe makers.

But that hasn't happened. My air fryer is still there, going strong, making tasty food, fast and healthy.

There was one thing missing though. Advice. As a fellow air fryer you'll know that the machine works in a unique way. It has its own quirks (I've never had to worry about my food being blown around before!) and its own benefits – but only if you know how to make full use of them.

I can remember being reliant on the recipes that came with the machine for a long time. They were OK. But the manufacturers are the experts at making the machine – not cooking the food.

Before too long I was desperate to try something new.

I started asking around at work – and discovered that other people were in the same position. They had the machine. They loved it. They could see its potential. But they didn't know whay to do next.

So, together, we began to experiment.

We tried swapping recipes, changing recipes, learning more about the possibilities.

Along the way we had some real disasters. *Real* disasters. But we learnt from them – and, as well as drawing up a list of new recipes to try, we drew up a list of things that the manual won't tell you.

Now we call them our pro tips – and I'm going to share them with you (along with six more tips to get the most out of your machine). So, if you want to know the truth about oil and your air fryer (which the manual *doesn't* come clean about), then this is the book for you.

If you want to know how often you should clean it (hint – it isn't every day – far from it), then this is the book for you.

If you want to know the one big mistake that too many cooks make when preparing their meals (and which stops them getting the crispy results they want) then this is the book for you.

Mostly, however, this is the book for you if you want to learn to cook simple, hassle free and delicious recipes each and every time.

Every single one of these recipes has been triple tested – because I know that it is rare that you are cooking for yourself alone. You need to know that the recipe will work right – first time.

So I've tried it. I've given it to a friend to try. And they've given it to a friend to try. If it didn't work for one of us, then it hasn't gone in. Period.

You can see at a glance how long your prep will take, how long the recipe will take including cooking time and how many people the dish will serve. Your air fryer is simple, so the recipes should be too, right?

We have tried to include a range of recipes – from the easy staples that you will want to cook over and over again (fries anyone?) to those for special occasions, such as soufflé (and yes, you really can make them perfectly in your air fryer).

So, grab a pen and paper and start making notes on what you want to try – because your air fryer journey starts over the page!

2 CRISPY SKIN POTATO WEDGES

PREP: 40 MIN | TOTAL: 1 HR 40 MIN | SERVES: 4

4 medium russet potatoes
1 cup water
3 tablespoons canola oil
1 teaspoon paprika
¼ teaspoon black pepper
¼ teaspoon salt
1. Scrub the potatoes under running water to clean. Boil potatoes in salted water for 40 minutes or until fork tender. Cool completely (approximately 30 minutes) in the refrigerator.

2. In a mixing bowl combine canola oil, paprika, salt and black pepper. Cut cooled potatoes into □uarters and lightly toss in the mixture of oil and spices. Preheat the AirFryer to 390°F.

Add half of the potato wedges to the cooking basket and place skin side down, being careful not to overcrowd. Cook each batch for 13-15 minutes or until golden brown.

3 FRENCH FRIES

PREP: 10 MIN | TOTAL: 1 HR | SERVES: 4

2 medium russet potatoes, peeled
1 tablespoon olive oil
1. Peel the potatoes and cut them into 1/2 inch by 3 inch strips. Soak the potatoes in water for at least 30 minutes, then drain thoroughly and pat dry with a paper towel.

2. Preheat the Airfryer to 330°F. Place the potatoes in a large bowl and mix in oil, coating the potatoes lightly. Add the potatoes to the cooking basket and cook for 5 minutes, until crisp. Remove from the basket and allow to cool on a wire rack.

3. Increase the temperature of the Airfryer to 390°F and add the pre-cooked potatoes back into the basket, cooking for another 10-15 minutes or until golden brown. Thicker cut potatoes will take longer to cook, while thinner cut potatoes will cook faster

4 POTATO CROQUETTES

PREP: 30 MIN | TOTAL: 45 MIN | SERVES: 4

FOR THE FILLING
2 medium russet potatoes, peeled and cubed
1 egg yolk
½ cup parmesan cheese, grated
2 tablespoons all-purpose flour
2 tablespoons chives, finely chopped
1 pinch salt
1 pinch black pepper
1 pinch nutmeg

FOR THE BREADING
2 tablespoons vegetable oil
1 cup all-purpose flour
2 eggs, beaten
½ cup breadcrumbs

1. Boil the potato cubes in salted water for 15 minutes. Drain and mash finely in a large bowl using a potato masher or ricer. Cool completely. Mix in the egg yolk, cheese, flour and chives.

Season with salt, pepper and nutmeg. Shape the potato filling into the size of golf balls and set aside.

2. Preheat the Airfryer to 390°F. Mix the oil and breadcrumbs and stir until the mixture becomes loose and crumbly. Place each potato ball into the flour, then the eggs and then the breadcrumbs and roll into a cylinder shape.

Press coating to croquettes to ensure it adheres. Place half of the croquettes into the cooking basket, cooking each batch for 7-8 minutes, or until golden brown.

5 POTATOES AU GRATIN

PREP: 10 MIN | TOTAL: 25 MIN | SERVES: 4

3 medium russet potatoes, peeled
¼ cup milk
¼ cup cream
1 teaspoon black pepper
½ teaspoon nutmeg
¼ cup Gruyère or semi-mature cheese, grated

1. Preheat the Airfryer to 390°F. Slice the potatoes wafer-thin. In a bowl, mix the milk and cream and season to taste with salt, pepper and nutmeg. Coat the potato slices with the milk mixture.

2. Transfer the potato slices to a 6-inch quiche pan and pour the rest of the cream mixture from the bowl on top of the potatoes. Distribute the cheese evenly over the potatoes. Place the quiche pan in the cooking basket and slide the basket into the Airfryer.

Set the timer to 15 minutes and bake the gratin until it is nicely browned.

6 ROSEMAY RUSSET POTATO CHIPS

PREP: 40 MIN | TOTAL: 1 HR 10 MIN | SERVES: 2

2 medium russet potatoes

1 tablespoon olive oil

1 teaspoon rosemary, chopped

1 pinch salt

1. Scrub the potatoes under running water to clean. Cut the potatoes lengthwise and peel into thin chips directly into a mixing bowl full of water. Soak the potatoes for 30 minutes, changing the water several times. Drain thoroughly and pat completely dry with a paper towel.

2. Preheat the Airfryer to 330°F. In a mixing bowl, toss the potatoes with olive oil. Place them into the cooking basket and cook for 30 minutes or until golden brown, shaking frequently to ensure the chips are cooked evenly. When finished and still warm, toss in a large bowl with rosemary

and salt.

7 BACON WRAPPED SHRIMP

PREP: 15 MIN | TOTAL: 35 MIN | SERVES: 4

1 pound tiger shrimp, peeled and deveined

1 pound bacon, thinly sliced, room temperature

1. Take one slice of bacon and wrap it around the shrimp, starting from the head and finishing at the tail. Return the wrapped shrimp to the refrigerator for 20 minutes.

2. Preheat the Airfryer to 390°F. Remove the shrimp from the refrigerator and add half of them to the cooking basket, cooking each batch for 5-7 minutes. Drain on a paper towel prior to serving.

8 CHEDDAR BACON CROQUETTES

PREP: 40 MIN | TOTAL: 50 MIN | SERVES: 6

FOR THE FILLING

1 pound sharp cheddar cheese, block
1 pound bacon, thinly sliced, room temperature

FOR THE BREADING
2 tablespoons olive oil 1 cup all-purpose flour
2 eggs, beaten
½ cup seasoned breadcrumbs

1. Cut the cheddar cheese block into 6 equally sized portions, approximately 1-inch x 1¾-inch each. Take two pieces of bacon and wrap them around each piece of cheddar, fully enclosing the cheese. Trim any excess fat. Place the cheddar bacon bites in the freezer for 5 minutes to firm. Do not freeze.

2. Preheat the Airfryer to 390°F. Mix the oil and breadcrumbs and stir until the mixture becomes loose and

crumbly. Place each cheddar block into the flour, then the eggs and then the breadcrumbs. Press coating to cro□uettes to ensure it sticks. Place the cro□uettes in the cooking basket and cook for 7-8 minutes - or until golden brown.

9 CRISPY FRIED SPRING ROLLS

PREP: 20 MIN | TOTAL: 25 MIN | SERVES: 4

FOR THE FILLING

4 oz. cooked chicken breast, shredded
1 celery stalk, sliced thin
1 medium carrot, sliced thin
½ cup mushrooms, sliced thin
½ teaspoon ginger, finely chopped
1 teaspoon sugar
1 teaspoon chicken stock powder

FOR THE SPRING ROLL WRAPPERS

1 egg, beaten
1 teaspoon cornstarch
8 spring roll wrappers
½ teaspoon vegetable oil

1. Make the filling. Place the shredded chicken into a bowl and mix with the celery, carrot and mushrooms. Add the

ginger, sugar and chicken stock powder and stir evenly.

2. Combine the egg with the cornstarch and mix to create a thick paste; set aside. Place some filling onto each spring roll wrapper and roll it up, sealing the ends with the egg mixture.

3. Preheat the Airfryer to 390°F. Lightly brush the spring rolls with oil prior to placing in the cooking basket. Fry in two batches, cooking each batch for 3-4 minutes or until golden brown. Serve with sweet chilli sauce or soy sauce.

10 CRAB CROQUETTES

PREP: 20 MIN | TOTAL: 35 MIN | SERVES: 6

FOR THE FILLING

1 pound lump crab meat
2 egg whites, beaten
1 tablespoon olive oil
¼ cup red onion, finely chopped
¼ red bell pepper, finely chopped
2 tablespoons celery, finely chopped
¼ teaspoon tarragon, finely chopped
¼ teaspoon chives, finely chopped
½ teaspoon parsley, finely chopped
½ teaspoon cayenne pepper
¼ cup mayonnaise
¼ cup sour cream

FOR THE BREADING

3 eggs, beaten
1 cup all-purpose flour
1 cup panko breadcrumbs

1 teaspoon olive oil
½ teaspoon salt

1. In a small sauté pan over a medium-high heat, add olive oil, onions, peppers, and celery. Cook and sweat until translucent, about 4-5 minutes. Remove from heat and set aside to cool.

2. In a food processor, blend the panko breadcrumbs, olive oil and salt to a fine crumb. In three separate bowls, set aside panko mixture, eggs and flour. Combine remaining ingredients: crabmeat, egg whites, mayonnaise, sour cream, spices and vegetables in a large mixing bowl.

3. Preheat Airfryer to 390°F. Mold crab mixture to size of golf balls, roll each in flour, then in egg and finally in panko. Press crumbs to croquettes to stick. Place croquettes in basket, being careful not to overcrowd. Cook each batch for 8-10 minutes or until golden brown.

11 FETA TRIANGLES

PREP: 20 MIN | TOTAL: 30 MIN | SERVES: 5

1 egg yolk
4 ounces feta cheese
2 tablespoons flat-leafed parsley, finely chopped
1 scallion, finely chopped
5 sheets of frozen filo pastry, defrosted
2 tablespoons olive oil
Ground black pepper to taste

1. Beat the egg yolk in a bowl and mix in the feta, parsley and scallion; season with pepper to taste. Cut each sheet of filo dough into three strips. Scoop a full teaspoon of the feta mixture on the underside of a strip of pastry. Fold the tip of the pastry over the filling to form a triangle, folding the strip in a zigzag manner until the filling is wrapped in a triangle. Repeat until all the filo and feta has been used.

2. Preheat the Airfryer to 390°F. Brush the filo with a little oil and place five triangles in the cooking basket. Slide the basket into the Airfryer and cook for 3 minutes or until golden brown. Repeat the process with the remaining feta

triangles and serve.

12 KOREAN BBQ SATAY

PREP: 15 MIN | TOTAL: 30 MIN | SERVES: 4

1 pound boneless skinless chicken tenders
½ cup low sodium soy sauce
½ cup pineapple juice
¼ cup sesame oil
4 garlic cloves, chopped
4 scallions, chopped
1 tablespoon fresh ginger, grated
2 teaspoons sesame seeds, toasted
1 pinch black pepper

1. Skewer each chicken tender, trimming excess meat or fat. Combine all other ingredients in a large mixing bowl. Add the skewered chicken to the bowl, mix well and refrigerate, covered, for 2-24 hours.

2. Preheat the Airfryer to 390°F. Pat chicken completely dry with a paper towel. Add half of the skewers to the cooking basket and cook each batch for 5-7 minutes.

13 JERK CHICKEN WINGS

PREP: 15 MIN | TOTAL: 30 MIN | SERVES: 4

1 pound boneless skinless chicken tenders
½ cup low sodium soy sauce
½ cup pineapple juice
¼ cup sesame oil
4 garlic cloves, chopped
4 scallions, chopped
1 tablespoon fresh ginger, grated
2 teaspoons sesame seeds, toasted
1 pinch black pepper

1. Skewer each chicken tender, trimming excess meat or fat. Combine all other ingredients in a large mixing bowl. Add the skewered chicken to the bowl, mix well and refrigerate, covered, for 2-24 hours.

2. Preheat the Airfryer to 390°F. Pat chicken completely dry with a paper towel. Add half of the skewers to the cooking basket and cook each batch for 5-7 minutes.

14 MOROCCAN MEATBALLS WITH MINT YOGURT

PREP: 25 MIN | TOTAL: 40 MIN | SERVES: 4

FOR THE MEATBALLS

1 pound ground lamb
4 ounces ground turkey
1½ tablespoons parsley, finely chopped
1 tablespoon mint, finely chopped
1 teaspoon ground cumin
1 teaspoon ground corriander
1 teaspoon cayenne pepper
1 teaspoon red chilli paste
2 garlic cloves, finely chopped
¼ cup olive oil
1 teaspoon salt
1 egg white

FOR THE MINT YOGURT

½ cup non-fat Greek yogurt
¼ cup sour cream

2 tablespoons buttermilk
¼ cup mint, finely chopped
1 garlic clove, finely chopped
2 pinches salt

1. Preheat the Airfryer to 390°F. In a large mixing bowl combine all ingredients for the meatballs. Roll the meatballs between your hands in a circular motion to smooth the meatball out to the size of a golf ball. Place half the meatballs into the cooking basket and cook each batch for 6-8 minutes.

2. While the meatballs are cooking add all of the ingredients for the mint yogurt to a medium mixing bowl and combine well. Serve with the meatballs and garnish with fresh mint and olives.

15 PIGS IN BLANKETS

PREP: 15 MIN | TOTAL: 30 MIN | SERVES: 4

1 12-ounce package cocktail franks
1 8-ounce can of crescent rolls

1. Remove the cocktail franks from the package and drain; pat dry on paper towels. Cut the dough into rectangular strips, approximately 1-inch x 1.5-inch. Roll the strips around the franks, leaving the ends visible. Place in the freezer for 5 minutes to firm.

2. Preheat the Airfryer to 330°F. Remove the franks from the freezer and place half of them in the cooking basket. Cook each batch for 6-8 minutes or until golden brown.

16 STUFFED GARLIC MUSHROOMS

PREP: 10 MIN | TOTAL: 20 MIN | SERVES: 4

12 button mushrooms

FOR THE STUFFING

1 slice of white bread
1 garlic clove, crushed 1 tablespoon flat-leafed parsley, finely chopped
Ground black pepper to taste
1 tablespoon olive oil

1. Preheat the Airfryer to 390°F. In a food processor, grind the slices of bread into fine crumbs and mix in the garlic, parsley and pepper to taste. When fully mixed, stir in the olive oil.

2. Cut off the mushroom stalks and fill the caps with the breadcrumbs. Pat crumbs into caps to ensure loose crumbs do not get pulled up into fan. Place the mushroom caps in

the cooking basket and slide it into the Airfryer. Cook the mushrooms for 10 minutes or until they are golden and crispy.

17 CHIMICHURRI SKIRT STEAK

ACTIVE: 15 MIN | TOTAL: 35 MIN | SERVES: 2

1 pound skirt steak

FOR THE CHIMICHURRI

1 cup parsley, finely chopped
¼ cup mint, finely chopped
2 tablespoons oregano, finely chopped
3 garlic cloves, finely chopped
1 teaspoon crushed red pepper
1 tablespoon ground cumin
1 teaspoon cayenne pepper
2 teaspoons smoked paprika
1 teaspoon salt
¼ teaspoon black pepper
¾ cup olive oil
3 tablespoons red wine vinegar

1. Combine the ingredients for the chimichurri in a mixing bowl. Cut the steak into 2 8-ounce portions and add to a re-sealable bag, along with ¼ cup of the chimichurri.

Refrigerate for 2 hours up to 24 hours. Remove from the refrigerator 30 minutes prior to cooking.

2. Preheat the Airfryer to 390°F. Pat steak dry with a paper towel. Add the steak to the cooking basket and cook for 8-10 minutes for medium-rare. Garnish with 2 tablespoons of chimichurri on top and serve.

18 ROASTED HEIRLOOM TOMATO WITH BAKED FETA

PREP: 20 MIN | TOTAL: 35 MIN | SERVES: 4

FOR THE TOMATO

1 heirloom tomato
1 8-ounce block of feta cheese
½ cup red onions, sliced paper thin
1 tablespoon olive oil
1 pinch salt

FOR THE BASIL PESTO

½ cup parsley, roughly chopped
½ cup basil, rough chopped
½ cup parmesan cheese, grated
3 tablespoons pine nuts, toasted
1 garlic clove
½ cup olive oil
1 pinch salt

1. Make the pesto. In a food processor, add parsley, basil, parmesan, garlic, toasted pine nuts and salt. Turn on the food processor and slowly add the olive oil. Once all of the olive oil is incorporated into the pesto, store and refrigerate until ready to use.

2. Preheat the Airfryer to 390°F. Slice the tomato and the feta into ½ inch thick circular slices.

Pat tomato dry with a paper towel. Spread 1 tablespoon of the pesto on top of each tomato slice and top with the feta. Toss the red onions with 1 tablespoon of olive oil and place on top of the feta.

3. Place the tomatoes/feta into the cooking basket and cook for 12-14 minutes or until the feta starts to soften and brown. Finish with a pinch of salt and an additional spoonful of basil pesto.

19 PORTABELLA PEPPERONI PIZZA

PREP: 5 MIN | TOTAL: 10 MIN | SERVES: 1

1 portabella mushroom cap, cleaned and scooped
1 tablespoon olive oil
1 tablespoon tomato sauce
1 tablespoon mozzarella, shredded
4 slices pepperoni
1 pinch salt
1 pinch dried Italian seasonings

1. Preheat the Airfryer to 330°F. Drizzle olive oil on both sides of the portabella, then season the inside of the portabella with salt and the Italian seasonings. Spread the tomato sauces evenly around the mushroom and then top with cheese.

2. Place the portabella into the cooking basket and slide into the Airfryer. After 1 minute, remove the cooking basket from the Airfryer and place the pepperoni slices on top of the portabella pizza. Cook for an additional 3 to 5

minutes. Finish with freshly grated parmesan cheese and crushed red pepper flakes.

20 MUSHROOM, ONION AND FETA FRITTATA

PREP: 15 MIN | TOTAL: 25 MIN | SERVES: 2

3 eggs
2 cups button mushrooms, cleaned
½ red onion
1 tablespoon olive oil
3 tablespoons feta cheese, crumbled
1 pinch salt

1. Peel and slice half a red onion into ¼ inch thin slices. Clean button mushrooms; then cut into ¼ inch thin slices. In a sauté pan with olive oil, sweat onions and mushrooms under a medium flame until tender. Remove from heat and place on a dry kitchen towel to cool.

2. Preheat the Airfryer to 330°F. In a mixing bowl crack 3 eggs and whisk thoroughly and vigorously, adding a pinch of salt. In a 6-ounce ramekin, coat the outside and bottom with a light coating of pan spray. Pour eggs into the ramekin, then the onion and mushroom mixture and then

the cheese.

Place the ramekin in the cooking basket and cook in the Airfryer for 10 to 12 minutes.

The frittata is done when you can stick a knife into the middle, and the knife comes out clean.

21 ROASTED CORNISH GAME HEN

ACTIVE: 15 MIN | TOTAL: 30 MIN | SERVES: 4

1 Cornish hen (approximately 2 pounds)

FOR THE MARINADE

½ cup olive oil
¼ teaspoon crushed red pepper flakes
1 teaspoon chopped thyme
1 teaspoon chopped rosemary
¼ teaspoon salt
¼ teaspoon sugar
zest of 1 lemon

1. Set the Cornish hen upright on a cutting board and with the back of the hen facing you, use a boning knife or a chef's knife to cut from the top of the back bone to the bottom of the back bone, making 2 cuts. Remove the back bone. Split the hen lengthwise, cutting through the breastplate. Take the two halves of the hen and set them

aside.

2. In a mixing bowl combine all ingredients for the marinade, then add the hens. Refrigerate for 1 hour up to 24 hours.

3. Preheat the Airfryer to 390°F. Remove the hens from the marinade, draining any additional li□uid with a strainer. Pat dry with a paper towel. Add the hens to the cooking basket and cook for 14-16 minutes or until the leg is at an internal temperature of 165°F.

22 SALMON WITH DILL SAUCE

PREP: 15 MIN | TOTAL: 25 MIN | SERVES: 2

FOR THE SALMON

12 ounces salmon
2 teaspoons olive oil
1 pinch salt

FOR THE DILL SAUCE

½ cup non-fat Greek yogurt
½ cup sour cream
1 pinch salt 2 tablespoons dill, finely chopped

1. Preheat the Airfryer to 270°F. Cut the salmon into two 6-ounce portions and drizzle 1 teaspoon of olive oil over each piece. Season with a pinch of salt. Place the salmon into the cooking basket and cook for 15-17 minutes.

2. Make the dill sauce. In a mixing bowl combine the yogurt, sour cream, chopped dill and salt. Top the cooked salmon with the sauce and garnish with an additional

pinch of chopped dill.

23 TERIYAKI GLAZED HALIBUT STEAK

PREP: 30 MIN | TOTAL: 39-41 MIN | SERVES: 3

1 pound halibut steak

FOR THE MARINADE:

2/3 cup soy sauce (low sodium)
½ cup mirin (Japanese cooking wine)
¼ cup sugar
2 tablespoons lime juice
¼ cup orange juice
¼ teaspoon crushed red pepper flakes
¼ teaspoon ginger ground
1 each garlic clove (smashed)

1. In a sauce pan combine all ingredients for the teriyaki glaze/marinade.

2. Bring to a boil and reduce by half, then cool.

3. Once cooled pour half of the glaze/marinade into a

resealable bag with the halibut.

4. Refrigerate for 30 minutes.

5. Preheat the Airfryer to 390°F.

6. Place the marinated halibut into the Airfryer and cook for 9-11 minutes.

7. When finished brush a little of the remaining glaze over the halibut steak.

8. Serve over a bed of white rice with basil/mint chutney.

24 CAJUN SHRIMP

PREP: 5 MIN | TOTAL: 10 MIN | SERVES: 2

½ pound tiger shrimp (16-20 count)
¼ teaspoon cayenne pepper
½ teaspoon old bay seasoning
¼ teaspoon smoked paprika
1 pinch of salt
1 tablespoon olive oil

1. Preheat the Airfryer to 390°F. In a mixing bowl combine all of the ingredients, coating the shrimp with the oil and the spices. Place the shrimp into the cooking basket and cook for 5 minutes. Serve over rice.

25 COD FISH NUGGETS

PREP: 15 MIN | TOTAL: 35 MIN | SERVES: 4

1 pound cod

FOR THE BREADING

2 tablespoons olive oil
1 cup all-purpose flour
2 eggs, beaten
¾ cup panko breadcrumbs
1 pinch salt

1. Preheat the Airfryer to 390°F. Cut the cod into strips approximately 1-inch by 2.5-inches in length. In a food processor, blend the panko breadcrumbs, olive oil and salt to a fine crumb. In three separate bowls, set aside the panko mixture, eggs and flour.

2. Place each piece of cod into the flour, then the eggs and then the breadcrumbs. Press the fish firmly into breadcrumbs to ensure they stick to the fish. Shake off any excess breadcrumbs. Add half of the cod nuggets to the

cooking basket, cooking each batch for 8-10 minutes or until golden brown.

26 COUNTRY CHICKEN TENDERS

PREP: 15 MIN | TOTAL: 35 MIN | SERVES: 4

1 pound chicken tenders

FOR THE BREADING

3 eggs, beaten
½ cup seasoned breadcrumbs
½ cup all-purpose flour
½ teaspoon salt
1 teaspoon black pepper
2 tablespoons olive oil

1. Preheat the Airfryer to 330°F. In three separate bowls, set aside the breadcrumbs, eggs and flour. Season the breadcrumbs with salt and pepper. Add olive oil to the breadcrumbs and mix well. Place the chicken in the flour, then dip into the eggs and finally coat with the breadcrumbs. Press to ensure breadcrumbs are coated securely and evenly to the chicken.

Shake off any excess breading prior to placing in the

cooking basket. Cook half of the chicken tenders at a time, with each batch cooking for 10 minutes or until golden brown.

27 GRILLED CHEESE

PREP: 10 MIN | TOTAL: 15 MIN | SERVES: 2

4 slices of brioche or white bread
½ cup sharp cheddar cheese
½ cup butter, melted

1. Preheat the Airfryer to 360°F. Place cheese and butter in separate bowls. Brush the butter on each side of the 4 slices of bread. Place the cheese on 2 of the 4 pieces of bread. Put the grilled cheese together and add to the cooking basket. Cook for 4-5 minutes or until golden brown and the cheese has melted.

28 MINI CHEESEBURGER SLIDERS

PREP: 5 MIN | TOTAL: 15 MIN | SERVES: 2

8 ounces ground beef
2 slices cheddar cheese
2 dinner rolls
salt
black pepper

1. Preheat the Airfryer to 390°F. Form the ground beef into 2 x 4-ounce patties and season with salt and pepper. Add the burgers to the cooking basket and cook for 10 minutes. Remove from the Airfryer; place the cheese on top of the burgers and return to the Airfryer to cook for one more minute.

29 PEANUT BUTTER MARSHMALLOW FLUFF TURNOVERS

PREP: 15 MIN | TOTAL: 20 MIN | SERVES: 4

4 sheets filo pastry, defrosted
4 tablespoons chunky peanut butter
4 teaspoons marshmallow fluff
2 ounces butter, melted
1 pinch sea salt

1. Preheat the Airfryer to 360°F. Brush 1 sheet of filo with butter. Place a second sheet of filo on top of the first and also brush with butter. Repeat until you have used all 4 sheets. Cut the filo layers into four 3-inch x 12-inch strips.

2. Place 1 tablespoon of peanut butter and 1 teaspoon of marshmallow fluff on the underside of a strip of filo. Fold the tip of the sheet over the filling to form a triangle and fold repeatedly in a zigzag manner until the filling is fully wrapped. Use a touch of butter to seal the ends of the

turnover. Place the turnovers into the cooking basket and cook for 3-5 minutes, until golden brown and puffy. Finish with a touch of sea salt for a sweet and salty combination.

30 VANILLA SOUFFLE

ACTIVE: 20 MIN | TOTAL: 1 HR 30 MIN | SERVES: 4

¼ cup all-purpose flour
¼ cup butter, softened
1 cup whole milk
¼ cup sugar
2 teaspoons vanilla extract
1 vanilla bean
5 egg whites
4 egg yolks
1 ounce sugar
1 teaspoon cream of tartar

1. Mix the flour and butter until it is a smooth paste. In a saucepan heat the milk and dissolve the sugar. Add the vanilla bean and bring to a boil. Add the flour and butter mixture to the boiling milk. With a wire whisk, beat vigorously to ensure there are no lumps. Simmer for several minutes until the mix thickens. Remove from the

heat, discard the vanilla bean and cool for 10 minutes in an ice bath.

2. While the mix is cooling, take six 3-ounce ramekins or soufflé dishes. Coat with butter and sprinkle with a pinch of sugar. In another mixing bowl □uickly beat the egg yolks and vanilla extract and combine with the milk mixture.

3. Separately beat the egg whites, sugar and cream of tartar until the egg whites form medium stiff peaks. Fold the egg whites into the soufflé base and pour into the prepared baking dishes and smooth off the tops.

4. Preheat the Airfryer to 330°F. Place 2 or 3 soufflé dishes into the cooking basket and cook each batch for 12-15 minutes. Serve with powdered sugar on top of the soufflé and with chocolate sauce on the side.

31 BLOOMING ONION

PREP: 15 MIN | TOTAL: 30 MIN | SERVES: 4

1 large white onion
¼ cup milk, nonfat
2 large eggs
¾ cup Panko
1 ½ teaspoon paprika
1 garlic powder
½ teaspoon cajun seasoning
½ teaspoon black pepper
1 teaspoon sea salt

Mix breadcrumbs with olive oil and cajun seasoning. In a separate dish, mix salt & pepper into the our. In a bowl, mix milk with egg.

Peel onion, cut off top. Place cut side down onto a cutting board. Starting 12 inch from the root, cut downward, all the way to the cutting board. Repeat to make 4 evenly spaced cuts around the onion. Continue slicing between each section until you have made 8 cuts in total.

Place sliced onion in ice water for at least 2 hours / overnight. Remove from water, pat dry. Open onion. Beat eggs with 2 tbsp. milk. Place onion on a tray or in a bowl.

Sprinkle onion generously with mixture. Make sure to get in between all. Turn onion upside down to remove excess.

Using a ladle, ladle the egg mixture into every crevice. Lift up onion and turn to make sure excess egg drips off. Sprinkle onion very generously with bread crumb mixture. Press into place.

Place the blooming onion into the fry basket and cook at 360F with foil on. When timer is done, check crispness of the onion. Cook 5-10 more minutes to desired crispness.

32 CRISPY JALAPENO POPPERS

PREP: 10 MIN | TOTAL: 20 MIN | SERVES: 1

2 Jalapeno Peppers
1 ounce cheddar cheese
1 spring roll wrapper
1 tablespoon egg beaters or egg creations (original)

Prepare the peppers: chop stem end off, slice lengthwise, trim out inner white pith and all seeds. Pat dry and set aside, trying to keep matching halves together.

Divide the cheese into 2 x ½ oz (15 g) strips.

Peel off a sheet of spring roll wrapper, and cut in half. Brush each half with half a tablespoon of the li□uid egg mixture, particularly the edges.

Place a half of jalapeño in one corner of the spring roll wrapper half (egg-brushed side up) as shown, place a strip of cheese in the cavity, and top with the other half of that jalapeño pepper.

Holding the two halves of the pepper together, roll the pepper up tightly in the springroll wrapper on the diagonal, folding the edges in.

When done, do a quick check for any loose edges of wrapper - glue any found down tightly with a quick brush of the egg.

When all are assembled, give each popper a very light spray with cooking spray. Turn over, spray the other side lightly.

Place in airfryer. You can fit a max of about 8 at a time in.

Turn Actifry / Airfryer on for 10 minutes, at which point they will be done. There's no need to turn them during cooking. You may wish to give them another minute or two to brown them further, depending on the phase of the moon and how well they browned.

33 SWEET POTATO FRIES

PREP: 5 MIN | TOTAL: 30 MIN | SERVES: 2

1 kg (2.2 lbs / 2 large) sweet potatoes
1 tablespoon oil

Wash the sweet potatoes. Peel. Cut into fries / chips. Put into a large bowl.

Add the 1 tablespoon of oil to the bowl and just using your clean hands, toss well until all surfaces of the potato are coated.

Cook (no need to pre-heat machine) at 320F for 15 minutes.

Take out the fries and tip them back into the bowl you have been using. Toss them in there briefly and gently using a large spoon, or just by tossing the bowl.

Transfer fries back into fryer basket. Place back into machine, raise temperature on the machine to 350F, and cook for another 5 minutes.

Take out the fries and tip them back into the bowl you have been using. Toss them in there using a large spoon. (At this point, a few might look just about done, but once you toss them you'll see that there's loads that aren't □uite as far along.)

Transfer fries back into fryer basket. Leave temperature unchanged. Roast for a final 5 minutes. Serve piping hot.

34 ZUCCHINI WEDGES

PREP: 10 MIN | TOTAL: 24 MIN | SERVES: 4

½ cup panko crumbs
¼ cup grated parmesan
¼ teaspoon basil
¼ teaspoon oregano
¼ teaspoon cayenne pepper
¼ cup egg white (about 2 egg whites)
2 medium-sized zucchini

In a bowl, mix together the crumbs, cheese and herbs, set aside. Wash the zucchini well; leave unpeeled. Cut in half cross wise, then cut into wedges not more than 1 cm (1/2 inch) thick.

Put egg white in a shallow bowl or place. Put a small amount of the crumb mixture on another plate. Dip a zucchini wedge in the egg white to coat, then in the crumbs to coat, pressing down well – before placing in Air Fryer. Repeat till all wedges are coated.

Spray lightly the wedges. Cook for 7 minutes; with tongs turn them over, and cook for another 7 minutes.

35 BAKED BUFFALO WINGS

PREP: 10 MIN | TOTAL: 35 MIN | SERVES: 2

Chicken wings
Self-raising flour
½ cup Frank's Hot Sauce
½ cup butter
1 tsp salt

Preheat your air fryer to 350°F. Take your chicken wings and cut the tip off. Put the chicken wings in a medium/large bowl and coat them with flour and salt.

Transfer the chicken wings to the basket of your air fryer and shake very well. Place the basket in the air fryer for 25 minutes. It's important to shake the chicken wings every 5 minutes.

Make the sauce. Simply melt the butter on medium heat and mix with the Frank's Hot Sauce. Remove the chicken wings from the basket and into a large bowl. Pour the sauce over the chicken wings and give them a good mix.

36 HONEY BARBECUE CHICKEN WINGS

PREP: 5 MIN | TOTAL: 26 MIN | SERVES: 2

Chicken wings
Salt and pepper
½ cup of flour
BBQ sauce of your choice
Honey

Preheat the air fryer to 350°F. Cut the chicken wings into three pieces. Discard the tip of the wings. Place them in a bowl and mix with flour, salt and pepper.

Place the chicken wings in the basket of your air fryer and □□□cook for 8 minutes. Shake the basket and cook for another 5 minutes at 400°F to achieve the crispiness.

Mix the barbecue sauce with honey and paint the wings with a cooking brush. Cook for 5 more minutes at 350°F. Give the chicken wings a good shake and coat them with the sauce again. Now cook them for 3 minutes.

37 MARINATED CHICKEN WINGS

PREP: 40 MIN | TOTAL: 60 MIN | SERVES: 2

Chicken wings
½ cup olive oil
1 tsp hot paprika, or sweet paprika
Pepper and salt

Preheat air fryer to 400°F. Mix ½ cup of olive oil, paprika, salt and pepper in a bowl. Add the chicken wings to the mixture and let them marinate for about 30-60 minutes.

Put the chicken wings in a basket and set the timer of your air fryer to 12 minutes. Shake the basket to allow the chicken wings to cook from all sides. Set the timer to another 8 minutes. Remove the chicken wings from the basket and serve on a plate.

38 GARLIC PARMESAN CHICKEN WINGS

PREP: 5 MIN | TOTAL: 30 MIN | SERVES: 2

2 pounds of frozen chicken wings
¼ cup grated parmesan cheese
¼ cup butter
2 minced garlic cloves
1 tsp rosemary
1 tsp oregano
½ tsp salt
¼ tsp paprika

Preheat your air fryer to 400°F. Fry the chicken wings for 24 minutes.

For the sauce, melt the butter and add garlic. Cook on medium heat for couple of minutes. Mix the spices and herbs together and add them to sauce. When chicken wings are cooked, pour the sauce over them.

Top everything with parmesan cheese, serve and enjoy.

39 DRY RUB CHICKEN

PREP: 5 MIN | TOTAL: 20 MIN | SERVES: 2

Chicken wings (14 pieces)
½ tsp salt
1 tsp garlic powder
1 tsp chili powder
½ tsp black pepper

Mix the garlic powder, chili powder, salt and pepper in a bowl. Add the chicken wings and mix until they're all coated. Put your wings in the basket of an air fryer and cook at 350°F for 15 minutes.

40 AIR FRYING PRO TIPS

Air fryers have come to change the idea of cooking. They're fun, healthier (depending on what you cook, of course!) and not too expensive when compared to other large electric cooking devices. They also save significantly on oil use, which is good for both your arteries and your wallet

Make sure you find the right place for your air fryer in your kitchen. Always keep your air fryer on a level, heat-resistant countertop and make sure there are at least five inches of space behind the air fryer where the exhaust vent is located.

Pre-heat your air fryer before adding your food. This is easy – just turn the air fryer on to the temperature that you need and set the timer for 2 or 3 minutes. When the timer goes off, the air fryer has pre-heated and is ready for food.

Invest in a kitchen spray bottle. Spraying oil on the food is easier than drizzling or brushing, and allows you to use less oil overall. While you can buy oil sprays in cans, sometimes there are aerosol agents in those cans that can break down the non-stick surface on your air fryer basket. So, if you want to spray foods directly in the basket, invest in a hand-pumped kitchen spray bottle. It will be worth it!

Use the proper breading technique. Breading is an important step in many air fryer recipes. Don't skip a step! It is important to coat foods with flour first, then egg and then the breadcrumbs.

Be diligent about the breadcrumbs and press them onto the food with your hands. Because the air fryer has a powerful fan as part of its mechanism, breading can sometimes blow off the food. Pressing those crumbs on firmly will help the breading stick.

Get the right accessories. Once you start air frying, you may want to invest in some accessories for your new favorite appliance. Truth is, you may already have some!

Any baking dishes or cake pans that are oven-safe should be air fryer-safe as well, as long as they don't come in contact with the heating element. The only stipulation, of course, is that the accessory pan has to be able to fit inside the air fryer basket.

Use an aluminum foil sling. Getting accessory pieces into and out of the air fryer basket can be tricky. To make it easier, fold a piece of aluminum foil into a strip about 2-inches wide by 24-inches long. Place the cake pan or baking dish on the foil and by holding the ends of the foil, you'll be able to lift the pan or dish and lower it into the air fryer basket.

Fold or tuck the ends of the aluminum foil into the air fryer basket, and then return the basket to the air fryer.

When you're ready to remove the pan, unfold and hold onto the ends of the aluminum foil to lift the pan out of the air fryer basket.

While You Are Air-Frying

Add water to the air fryer drawer when cooking fatty foods. Adding water to the drawer underneath the basket helps prevent grease from getting too hot and smoking. Do this when cooking bacon, sausage, even burgers if they are particularly fatty.

Use toothpicks to hold foods down. Every once in a while, the fan from the air fryer will pick up light foods and blow them around. So, secure foods (like the top slice of bread on a sandwich) with toothpicks.

Don't overcrowd the basket. I can't stress this enough. It's tempting to try to cook more at one time, but over-crowding the basket will prevent foods from crisping and browning evenly and take more time over all.

Flip foods over halfway through the cooking time. Just as you would if you were cooking on a grill or in a skillet, you need to turn foods over so that they brown evenly.

Open the air fryer as often as you like to check for doneness. This is one of the best parts of air fryers – you can open that drawer as often as you like (within reason) to check to see how the cooking process is coming along. This will not interrupt the timing of most air fryers – the fryer will either continue heating and timing as you pull the basket out, or pick up where it left off when you return the basket to the fryer.

Shake the basket. Shaking the basket a couple of times during the cooking process will re-distribute the ingredients and help them to brown and crisp more evenly.

Spray with oil part way through. If you are trying to get the food to brown and crisp more, try spritzing it with oil part way through the cooking process. This will also help the food to brown more evenly.

After You Air-Fry

Remove the air fryer basket from the drawer before turning out foods. This is very important and it's a mistake you'll only make once.

If you invert the basket while it is still locked into the air fryer drawer, you will end up dumping all the rendered fat or excess grease onto your plate along with the food you just air-fried.

Don't pour away the juices from the drawer too soon. The drawer below the air fryer basket collects a lot of juices from the cooked foods above and catches any marinades that you pour over the food.

If the drippings are not too greasy, you can use this flavorful liquid as a sauce to pour over the food. You can also de-grease this li□uid and reduce it in a small saucepan on the stovetop for a few minutes to concentrate the flavor.

Clean the drawer as well as the basket after every use. The drawer of the air fryer is very easy to clean, so don't put it off. If you leave it unwashed, you'll run the risk of food contamination and your kitchen won't smell very nice in a day or so!

Use the air fryer to dry itself. After washing the air fryer basket and drawer, just pop them back into the air fryer and turn it on for 2 or 3 minutes. That dries both parts better than any drying towel.

Re-Heating Foods In The Air-Fryer

There's no hard and fast rule for time and temperature when re-heating leftovers because leftovers vary so significantly.

I suggest re-heating in the air fryer at 350°F and doing so for as long as it takes for the food to be re-heated to a food safety temperature of 165°F. This is especially important for any potentially hazardous foods like chicken, pork and beef.

Trouble-Shooting

The food isn't getting crispy enough. Make sure you are not over-crowding the air fryer basket and make sure you are using just a little oil.

There is white smoke coming from the air fryer. Add some water to the air fryer drawer underneath the basket. The white smoke is probably because grease has drained into the drawer and is burning. Adding water will prevent this.

There is black smoke coming from the air fryer. Turn the machine off and look up towards the heating element inside the fryer. Some food might have blown up and attached to the heating element, burning and causing the black smoke.

The air fryer won't turn off. Many air fryers are designed to have a delay in their shutting down process. Once you press the power button off, the fan will continue to blow the hot air out of the unit for about 20 seconds. Don't press the power button again, or you will have just turned the machine back on. Be patient and wait, and the air fryer will turn off.

41 SIX TRICKS TO GET MORE OUT OF YOUR AIR FRYER

Shake & Mix

When you are using lots of oil, the liquid helps your food to mix properly. That does not happen in air fryers as air is not strong enough to move the separate particles. Therefore, make sure that you are opening up the machine and mixing your food at least once when you are cooking.

A standard process that people use is rotating and mixing the food at the midway point. So for example, if you set your timer at ten minutes then you can pause the fryer at the fifth minute and mix the stuff around before you restart it again.

Keep It Light

A common mistake that many people make is overcrowding the air fryer. Deep frying helps you to understand how much food can actually be cooked at one go via full submersion in the oil. When there is no oil, you might not leave enough space for your ingredients to be cooked properly. Make sure that you do not fall for that mistake. Did you ever hear people complaining that their air fryers cannot provide crispy results? This is usually the reason. They don't leave enough space for the air flow and thus, half of their bowls don't get properly cooked. Refer to your model's instruction manual and ensure you aren't overloading the fryer.

Use Cooking Spray

They say you don't need oil but that is not the actual case. This is basically just a marketing strategy used to promote air fryers. In reality, you need to use a small amount of oil or cooking spray to make sure you are not losing taste.

Plus, cooking completely dry can cause some foods to get stuck to the fryer's surface – only a spray or a bit of oil can save you from that. So make sure you have cooking spray in your kitchen, especially for battered food that didn't come pre-oiled.

Stick To Natural Temperature

When working with fresh food, it's usually not a great idea to start cooking straight out of the fridge. Take your time and make sure the food you are putting into the dryer is at room temperature (but still fresh, of course.) This will cut down on cooking time and should lead to crisper results.

Try Stuff Other Than Frying

Though the name says 'air fryer', you should know that these gadgets can do a lot more than just frying food; you can cook everything from noodles to lasagna and even pizza. Indeed, the concept of the air fryer has more in common with a fan-forced oven than a deep fryer. We've even seen people cook soups using an air fryer. In other words, you should be experimental with it – just be sure to consult the manual before doing anything too adventurous.

Take Proper Care

Ultimately, make sure that you are taking good care of your air fryer. Air fryers do not need much love and attention but like an electronic appliance you do need to take care of it.

If you are cooking regularly with your air fryer, try to clean it at least once every fifteen days to make sure it stays odor and smell free. You can also use dishwasher if your fryer is dishwasher safe or has a removable basket.

42 SEVEN REASONS TO EAT MORE FOOD COOKED IN AN AIR FRYER

For many mere mortals, crispy fried food is their Kryptonite – it is high in harmful fat, but it tastes oh-so-good. While making smarter decisions on your food choices will benefit your health, there would be times when you just want that fried crunch. What to do?

Using healthier cooking methods are great to support a low-fat diet. Using an Air Fryer instead of a Deep Fryer will be a significant game changer to your diet and you will be able to eat fried food without feeling guilty.

Protect The Food's Nutrients

Unlike deep frying, Air Fryers do not deconstruct the food's good nutrients and add on bad fats. If you think your yasai tempura (deep fried battered vegetables) are healthy, here is news for you; while they may look like they are full of nutritious elements, the deep frying process would have destroyed the beneficial vitamins and minerals contained in the vegetables.

Keeping Cancer At Bay

For some oils (e.g. olive and flaxseed), their chemical structure changes in high heat causing them to transform into bad forms of fat. Additionally, since there is little oil used, there is little chances for food to produce carcinogens that activate cancer cells.

Calories Are Good, But Too Much Spells Trouble!

Fried foods are high in calories which is the leading cause of weight gain and obesity. Obesity will then lead to a plethora of killer diseases such as diabetes, cancer, stroke, sleep problems and immobility to name a few.

Adopting a low-fat diet will help you maintain your weight or prevent weight loss because essentially, you are eating fewer calories. Therefore, eating Air Fryer-cooked food will support your weight loss journey.

Build A Fortress For Your Heart

Eating food fried with an Air Fryer reduces the risk of heart diseases and protects your body by helping you absorb necessary nutrients. Since a minimal amount of oil is used to prepare food, you can be sure that your body will not accumulate excessive fats in the long run. Instead, the optimal amount of oil used will help your body protect your heart.

Keeping Your Kidneys Clear

Consuming excess amounts of deep-fried food will impair your kidney's ability to filter our harmful fats.

Therefore, eating food fried by an Air Fryer can help you lower your risks of getting kidney disease. If you are finding it difficult to quit deep-fried food cold turkey, using an Air Fryer will ease your transition to a healthier diet.

Fat Is Not All Bad

Fat is a macronutrient – it is essential to help control inflammation, blood clotting, maintaining healthy hair and skin, prevent heart diseases, provide energy and assist in the absorption of vitamins A, D, E and K. While it is important to your bodily functions, too much of it is detrimental to health.

An Air Fryer is a modern kitchen appliance that fries food using heated hot air by using at most a tablespoon of oil. This way, you are able to eat fried food without worrying about the negative effects of fatty food on your health.

43 THE SUPER QUICK HISTORY OF THE AIR FRYER

In 2010, Philips introduced the Airfryer, a new kitchen appliance at the Internationale Funkausstellung (IFA), an important consumer electronics fair in Berlin.

The AirFryer is an egg-shaped device that allows consumers to fry a variety of foods conveniently and easily, including French fries, snacks, chicken, and meat, among many other foods.

The AirFryer was developed using the patented Rapid Air technology, which results in frying crispy fries that contain up to 80% less fat than a conventional fryer.

Because the device uses only air to fry the foods, it produces fewer smells and vapors than traditional frying, it is easy to clean and safe for daily use. The Airfryer was listed in the top five inventions of the 2010 IFA.

The Airfryer became a major commercial success: It was the number one brand in low-fat fryers in 2015. Managers originally thought that the Airfryer would sell well in Europe, but the real successes were booked in other continents due to the variety of food that could be fried with the Airfyer. Its versatility is one of its best selling points.

The market for low-fat fryers is growing rapidly but still has a large growth potential, as the awareness among consumers is still low.

HAS THIS BOOK HELPED YOU?

If this book has helped you then please consider leaving a review on Amazon.

It means other people are more likely to find it and read about the ways that they can get the best out of this amazing piece of equipment!

Thank you!

Printed in Great Britain
by Amazon

60174385R00051